Wynkyn de Worde
Father of Fleet Street

James Moran

Wynkyn de Worde Society
London

© 1960 James Moran

First edition 1960 (hardback)

Second (revised) edition 1976 (paperback)

Design and typography by Ron Costley

Map drawn by Anna Farr

Origination by the Shenval Press

London and Harlow

This 1987 reprint lithographed by

GPS Ltd, Watford, Herts

on Grosvenor Chater's Basingwerk Smooth Cartridge

and bound by Forward Bindery Ltd

London N5

Distributed for the Wynkyn de Worde Society

by Lund Humphries Publishers Ltd

c/o Book Publishing Development plc

16 Pembridge Road, London W11 3HL

ISBN 85331 388 1

Introduction

The Wynkyn de Worde Society was founded in the autumn of 1957, a month or two before publication of the first book filmset in Great Britain. 'Printing', therefore, still meant doing what Gutenberg did. (If you did what Senefelder did, you were a lithographer, not a printer.) Many still regarded printing as an ancient and picturesque trade : the word 'craft' was often heard. A pub named 'The Printer's Devil' was opened near Fleet Street, full of letterpress hardware. Whether any printers patronised it I cannot say, but the fact that hardheaded brewers thought it worth doing, exemplifies the romantic aura that surrounded 'the art and mystery of a printer' thirty years ago.

This romanticism was occasionally to be found even among people actually connected with printing, so Arthur Heighway was warmly supported at our inaugural meeting when he proposed that the Society be named after Wynkyn de Worde. He printed pretty badly from barely legible type, but he had a certain allure as 'The Father of Fleet Street'. If the Society had been founded thirty years later we should probably have had a snappier name : Interface 87 perhaps, or an incomprehensible acronym.

As it was, we were stuck with dear old Wynkyn, about whom many early members needed the facts. Until information was forthcoming, some were almost as ignorant as the policeman who called at the Society's first postal address to enquire about 'this Dutchman who has not registered as an alien'.

The required information was provided by James Moran in the first edition of this book (1960). Moran, a founder-member, was brought into printing journalism by Arthur Heighway, who engaged him as editor of *Printing News* and *Book Design and Production*. 'He revelled in this field and finally became very knowledgeable in it', wrote Heighway in his privately printed autobiography. His work as an editor was distinguished, and he had a number of important books to his credit including an unauthorised critique of Morison's typographic achievement that was stronger on scepticism than on adulation. He could, and regularly did, write an article or booklet at the drop of a hat. I do not know the circumstances in which this book was commissioned and all who might know are, alas, dead, but I have no doubt that James readily agreed to perform, and delivered the typescript on or before the due date. He wrote to me not long before his untimely death in 1978 'I think it better to write to a deadline or you are always making fiddling alterations . . . a great fault among the over-academic.' He was arguably the most erudite printing journalist of his time.

James Moran was the second chairman of the Society. The first edition of this book was printed by the first chairman, James Shand, at the Shenval Press. Therefore this account of one of London's first printers was written by a descendant (as he put it) of 'a long line of small bog-trotting Irish chieftains' and printed by a Glaswegian removed to Hereford, using a German press and Welsh paper. There was a second edition in 1976. A condensed version was very lavishly circulated at the time of the 'Printing and the Mind of Man' exhibitions in 1963. Nevertheless, the Society's name is frequently misspelt, even occasionally on its own menu.

Bernard Roberts
Wendover, 1987

Preface

When I wrote this book in late 1959 the area around Fleet Street was indeed the home of most national newspapers and periodicals and provincial and overseas newspapers had their offices there. Many changes have occurred over sixteen years and Fleet Street is not what it was. But the words are still used to imply the popular press and so I have not altered my first words in Chapter One.

The book was one of my earlier literary efforts and in this new edition I have tried to clean up any blemishes it contained and to add some further information. Although I believe I would write the book rather differently if I were tackling it for the first time, I hope this refurbished work of my apprentice hand will prove acceptable to the members of the Wynkyn de Worde Society, with the founding of which I had so much to do, and those others in the printing industry who may receive a copy.

James Moran
London, 1976

Illustrations

The decoration facing the title page, and that
on page 47, are from de Worde's device which
depicts a sagittary, a greyhound and the sun.

*The illustrations on pages 21 and 38 are Crown
Copyright and are reproduced by permission of the
Controller of HM Stationery Office.*

Chapter One

'Fleet Street' has a wider connotation than that of the mere London street running from Ludgate Circus to the Strand. Because most national newspapers and many periodicals are produced in the street and its environs and provincial and overseas newspapers have their offices there, the words have come to imply, by extension, the popular press itself.

It is generally agreed that the man who brought printing to Fleet Street was William Caxton's assistant, Wynkyn de Worde, in about the year 1500. He was a native of the Duchy of Lorraine and is thought to have been born in the town of Wörth. This small town was eventually absorbed into France and is now in the Rhine Palatinate of Germany. Writing in the period immediately before the 1914–18 war the authority on early printers, E. Gordon Duff, often refers to de Worde as a 'German' by birth, no doubt because Wörth was then in Germany. William Blades, Caxton's biographer, refers to de Worde as a native of Belgium. But de Worde was not a Frenchman, a German or a Belgian, but a subject of the Duke of Lorraine. He was presumably born in the reign of Duke René, and died in that of Duke Anthony the Good, still a Lotharingian, as he had never become fully naturalised in England. Lorraine did not become fully incorporated into the Kingdom of France until 1766.

De Worde was followed into Fleet Street by Richard Pynson, Henry VII's printer, who was succeeded at the sign of St George, by Chancery Lane corner, by Richard Redman, although the office of King's Printer went to another Fleet Street printer, Thomas Berthelet.

Other early printers gathered about Fleet Street: John Notary, John Wayland, John Butler, Robert Copland and Richard Tottel, for example. They began the tradition of printing in Fleet Street, which has continued to this day.

De Worde, however, was not just a pioneer in a humble mechanical way of the great presses of Fleet Street. By his appreciation of the public's requirements he was also the forerunner of the popular press lords and hence the father of Fleet Street in its wider sense.[1]

From the Rhineland to England

But how did he get to England from the Rhineland and eventually assume his important rôle in the history of publishing? He was clearly brought over by Caxton, England's first printer, but where he met Caxton is a matter of speculation. Caxton learned the art of printing in Cologne. He practised it in Bruges, and brought it to Westminster, working near the Abbey. Here he rented various shops and tenements from 1476 onwards, and in 1482 the house near the Almonry where he hung out a heraldic sign, the 'Red pale'. The details of Caxton's houses at Westminster have been given by Lawrence E. Tanner, Keeper of the Abbey muniments, in *The Library*, fifth series, Vol. XIII, No. 3.

1 De Worde was not London's first printer. That honour goes to Joannes Lettou, who introduced the art of printing into London in 1480. Then, as now, London and Westminster were separate cities. Lettou was joined by William de Machlinia, a native of Malines (Mechelin) in Belgium, but then the residence of the Great Council and Margaret of York, the young Duchess of Burgundy. Their partnership broke up about 1483 and Machlinia began to work alone. He writes of himself as living near the 'Flete-Bridge' and he printed eight books there before moving to Holborn. He seems to have ceased printing by about 1490. He did not actually print in Fleet Street proper and was responsible for about only thirty publications, most of which were theological, scholastic or law books. He therefore cannot challenge de Worde either in the geographical or metaphorical sense as 'Father of Fleet Street'.

In an epilogue to the English translation of the *De proprietatibus rerum*, by Bartholomaeus Anglicus, printed by de Worde, there appear these lines:

> And also of your charyte call to remembraunce
> The soule of William Caxton, first prynter of this boke
> In laten tonge at Coleyn, hymself to avaunce
> That every well disposyd man may theron loke

E. Gordon Duff in his book *The Printers Stationers and Bookbinders of Westminster and London from 1476 to 1535* (Cambridge, 1906) writes: 'Now this is a perfectly clear statement that Caxton printed a Bartholomaeus in Latin at Cologne, and we know an edition of the book manifestly printed at Cologne about the time Caxton was there.'

In *Evidence that the first English printer learned his craft at Cologne* (London, 1928) Henry Thomas, Deputy Keeper of the Printed Books, British Museum, mentions Caxton's own remark in the preface of *Recuyell of the Historyes of Troye* that he finished his translation 'in the holy cyte of Colen', and the fact that Wynkyn de Worde also asserted that Caxton learned to print in Cologne.

Thomas writes: 'The *De proprietatibus rerum* must have been one of Caxton's favourite books of reference. It is quite natural that we should learn about his share in the printing of the editio princeps from his servant and successor Wynkyn de Worde', and 'We may take it that Wynkyn de Worde's edition realised an unachieved ambition of Caxton's, hence the verses at the end, with their loving recollection of his late master, and their perhaps slightly exaggerated reference to the part he took in the original edition, in order to train himself in the art of printing'. He concludes: 'We could hardly desire a better witness than Wynkyn de Worde, for he joined Caxton not more than eight years, perhaps as few as four, after the printing of the original edition.'

But Wynkyn de Worde's testimony has been questioned (notably by Blades), and Thomas therefore re-publishes evidence from the Cologne

Aliens Register which shows that Caxton received four permits to reside in the city for successive periods during 1471 and 1472. 'He was there throughout the period during which the editio princeps of Bartholomew's encyclopaedia, the product of a Cologne press, was being printed. Wynkyn de Worde's statement that Caxton took part in the printing is fully substantiated; he supplies us with Caxton's purpose, and we can now safely assert that Caxton learned the art of printing in Cologne.'

Caxton left Cologne some time during the latter half of 1472. Before returning to England he spent some four years in the Netherlands, setting up his own press in Bruges. He was back in England in 1476.

Since printing was unknown in England it is obvious that he had to find assistants in Europe and he may have come across de Worde when in Cologne or district.

Henry R. Plomer in *Wynkyn de Worde and his contemporaries* (London, 1925) says that in all probability de Worde came over to England with William Caxton, and at Caxton's solicitation as his assistant in 1476, or, if he did not actually travel with him, he must have followed Caxton almost immediately.

It is fairly clear that de Worde was a native of Wörth, as he sometimes called himself de Worth instead of de Worde. In his letter of denization he is described as a native of the Duchy of Lorraine. In de Worde's time the Duchies of Lorraine and Burgundy spread over into parts of what are now Belgium, France and Germany. Wörth is on the Rhine, only some 60 miles from Mainz, the birthplace of printing, and 140 miles from Cologne.

It seems likely that the young de Worde would have taken up an apprenticeship in the new art in the Rhineland, where it flourished, rather than to travel more than 200 miles to Bruges, where the art of printing was not known until Caxton and Colard Mansion, a calligrapher, began practising it in the fourteen-seventies.

The first definite record we have of de Worde's presence in England is a deed among the muniments of Westminster Abbey, dated 1480. This shows that he was married and that his wife Elizabeth had rented a house from the Prior previous to that date. His wife is presumed to have died in 1498. An entry for that year in the warden's accounts for St Margaret's, Westminster, reads:

> Item, for the knell of Elizabeth de Worde vi d
> Item, for iii torches, with the grete bell for her viii d.

The same account book for 1500 suggests that he may also have had a son:

> Item, for the knelle of Julian de Worde, with the grete bell vi d.

De Worde remained in Caxton's service for some fifteen years until the death of the latter in 1491. We know little about Caxton's family, except that he was married and had a daughter named Elizabeth, who was married to one Gerard Croppe, from whom she obtained a deed of separation in 1496. Had Caxton had a son he would have probably continued the printing business. As it was, the printing materials were inherited by his assistant, de Worde, who continued to work at Caxton's old house at Westminster.

E. G. Duff suggests that de Worde had very little enterprise to begin with as so few books are known to have been printed down to the end of 1493. Plomer gives a better explanation. He says Croppe seems to have been an ill-tempered man, and immediately on Caxton's death put forward a claim against the printer's estate, which his executors, one of whom was probably de Worde, would not entertain. Croppe started a series of actions against the executors and it may well be that this litigation delayed the proving of Caxton's will, which might have led to the stagnation of the printing business.

'This seems to be the most natural explanation of the drop in the output of books from the Red Pale in the years immediately following Caxton's death. That it was not due to any want of energy on de Worde's part is shown from the fact that before the close of the fifteenth century he printed more than one hundred books, in other words, when Caxton's affairs were settled up and the business was legally handed over to him, de Worde more than made up for the lost time', writes Plomer.

De Worde took over Caxton's house in Westminster, being duly entered in the rent roll of Abbot Esteney as the tenant. In 1494 in a poem at the end of *Scala Perfectionis* he tells how he had it 'sett in prynt / In Willyam Caxtons hows . . .'. Late in 1500 or early 1501 he moved from the sign of the Red Pale in Westminster to Fleet Street, to a house opposite Shoe Lane, at the sign of the Sun.

Caxton was the first Englishman to import printed books and his business at Westminster was that of a bookseller, conveniently near his prospective customers in the Court and Government. He sold books both imported and from his own press. De Worde carried this on and a fragment, described by William A. Jackson in *The Colophon*, New Series, No. 4, Vol. I, is probably a list of de Worde's transactions.

De Worde's influence on publishing

While Caxton was a scholarly man, de Worde was a craftsman but shrewd enough to realise that there was a wider market for cheap publications than that visualised by Caxton.

His place in history is that of the first publisher and printer to popularise the products of the printing press. Duff calls him 'by far the most important and prolific of all the early English printers'.

In a handlist of de Worde's publications, 1492–1535, in his excellent book, *English Books and Readers 1475 to 1557* (Cambridge, 1952), H. S. Bennett lists 829 publications. This attempt to bring together a list of de Worde publications, whether still in existence or not, accepts the attributions of earlier biographers, cataloguers and others.

Mr Bennett points out that de Worde saw there was a possible market for early romances which were still in manuscript form and from time to time throughout his career he printed little quarto volumes, containing such famous romances as *Bevis of Hampton*, *Sir Degare* and *Ipomydon*, as well as a number of others, at least four of which are unique, and it is to de Worde's enterprise that we owe the first editions of some of the romances.

Infynite laude wyth thankynges many folde
I yelde to god me socouryng wyth his grace
This boke to finyslhe whiche that ye beholde
Scale of perfeccion calde in every place
Wherof thaucto walter hilton was
And wynkyn de worde this hath sett in prynt
In willyam Carlstons hows so fyll the cale
God relt his soule. In Joy ther mot it ltynt

This heuenly boke more precyous than golde
was late dired wyth great humylyte
For godly plesur.theron to beholde
Onto the right noble Margaret as ye see
The kyngis moder of excellent bounte.
Henry the seuenth that Jhu hym preserue
This myghty pryncesle hath comaunded me
Temprynt this boke her grace for to delerue

Finit felicit liber intitulatus
Scala perfeccionis inprellus   año salutis. M. cccc. lxxxxiiii.

Poem at end of *Scala Perfectionis* showing that de Worde printed
this book at the command of the King's mother

'No one else showed so keen an interest in this field, although some decades later W. Copland found the market still brisk enough for him to print editions of a dozen or more romances between 1548 and 1557', writes Mr Bennett.

Another paragraph is worth quoting to indicate de Worde's position: 'Caxton's two chief successors, Wynkyn de Worde and Richard Pynson, seem to have shown little of his anxiety to find a patron. Each of them, it is true, published a limited number of books with the support of influential people, but on the whole they relied on their skill in judging what the public wanted. Other publishers, both contemporary and later, were seemingly not so confident of their powers in judging the potential market; and, as a result throughout the period, many printers were influenced by the wishes or instructions of patrons who were responsible for the work in some way or another.'

De Worde published outline histories for those who could not afford longer works. By publishing for a penny or two he anticipated the popular press lords of several centuries later. He understood the appeal of 'sensational' news, too, importing a broadside, for example, from Germany describing a 'horryble monster . . . cast of a Sowe' in Prussia. After experimenting in the first years of the sixteenth century he saw how to proceed and determined the main lines of his output for the next thirty years. Mr Bennett outlines the programme as follows: 'Briefly it was to give the public a variety of books on subjects known to have a popular appeal – religious and homiletic, practical and instructional – and to issue these in easily handled volumes likely to attract readers who would recoil from large and expensive volumes.'

He produced children's books, instructions for pilgrims, and works on good manners, marriage (from a number of points of view), household practice, medicines for horses, names of gods and goddesses, and husbandry.

The *Demaundes Joyous*, a nursery book, printed in 1510, contained such riddles as: 'How many cow's tails would it take to reach the moon?', with the answer: 'One – if it were long enough!'

Chapter Two

Fleet Street has not always been connected with printing. When de Worde went there it was a 'suburb' of the City of London with many large gardens and some open meadow land. The main characteristic of the street was ecclesiastical. By the time of the Reformation most of the land and property in and around Fleet Street was owned or rented by the many bishops and abbots whose sees or abbeys were situated in distant parts of England. These town houses of the clergy were the larger establishments standing well back in their own grounds, but the houses of the tradesmen, which fringed the street, were much smaller and often very mean. One of the earliest trades in Fleet Street was that of cap making, the cap makers having received their regulations in the reign of Henry III. The taverners also flourished and Fleet Street's reputation was that of a place given to drinking and carousing and convivial life long before the journalists and printers arrived.

De Worde must have been better off than most tradesmen, or was a better business man, for he occupied two houses near St Bride's church, one a dwelling house and the other a printing house, for which he paid the high tithe rent of sixty-six shillings and eight pence.

Why he moved there is not definitely known, but it is easy to conjecture that the Westminster office had become too small for a growing business and also that he wanted to be near the centre of the bookselling trade which then, and for many years afterwards, was settled about St Paul's churchyard.

Indeed, in addition to his printing house at the sign of the Sun, he had for a time, a bookseller's shop in St Paul's churchyard with the sign of Our Lady of Pity. Of course, the very ecclesiastical nature of Fleet Street may have attracted him. Churchmen provided a major market for books.

It is probable, as was the custom of the time, that he kept a stall in front of his shop in Fleet Street. As far as we can ascertain, the shop, with the sign of the Sun, stood approximately where Barclays Bank on the north-west corner of Salisbury Court stands today.

Looking across the road de Worde would see the inns or town houses and gardens of various ecclesiastics, including that of the Abbot of Peterborough (giving its name to Peterborough Court now running under the *Daily Telegraph* building). His servants would have obtained water from the conduit which stood out in the street where Shoe Lane enters.

The conduit was centuries old by de Worde's time, but Sir William Eastfield, mayor in 1438, had erected a standard for water supply at the entrance of Shoe Lane into Fleet Street. It was re-built by local inhabitants in 1478. It was an imposing structure – a stone tower over the cistern, with images of angels and St Christopher on it, and with 'sweet sounding bells' operated by an engine, which told the time by the chiming of hymns.

Also across the road was an estate known as the Popinjay, the site and name of which are preserved in Poppins Court. This was the town hostel of the Abbot and Convent of Cirencester, in Gloucestershire. But by de Worde's time the Abbot was in the habit of leasing it to tradesmen.

Down an alleyway to the rear of de Worde's house was the Bishop of Salisbury's house and garden and the St Bride's church, where de Worde worshipped and where he was buried.

St Bride's may have been small compared with Sir Christopher Wren's later building, but it had been enlarged by the benefactions of William Venor, a former Warden of the Fleet, who about the year 1480 added a nave and side aisles.

The Fleet Street of de Worde's day must not be visualised as a straight paved road. The houses rambled all over the place, rather like those of an old country village. Its worst characteristics, which de Worde would have had to put up with, were noise, smells and filth. He would have been wakened by the sounds of the miniature inland port not far from his house, and may have been disturbed by the clamour all day long of the bells of the many churches clustered together in one square mile, not to mention the chimes of the conduit, the cries of the street traders and the shouts arising from the many fights which seemed to take place. The insanitary habits of the people made the street and the river repositories of filth and from time to time complaints were made to the authorities (without much result it seems) about the stench of the tanneries crowded round the river. But the outcry from the citizens became sufficiently loud in 1501 for the river to be cleansed and scoured down to the Thames. Perhaps Master de Worde was one of these who complained. In any case the results were beneficial, for boats with oysters and herring rowed up the newly cleansed river and sold their wares as they had done of old. To citizens on a very restricted diet this would have been a pleasant change.

The Fleet river dominated the locality. There was a little bridge carrying Fleet Street over the river, and from beyond this rose the smell of reeking tanneries. Water was an essential for the industry and the tanners crowded towards the river, making the slip of land lying at the foot of London wall the headquarters for the preparation of hides for boots and saddlery. They were the men, with the cappers, whose trade was established long before the printing press came to make Fleet Street famous.

But there was one group, numerous in Shoe Lane, whose presence indicated the future development of the area. They were the bookbinders. There is a record of one Dionisia le Bokebyndere being robbed in her house in Fleet Street by five Welshmen in July 1311. So Fleet Street had connections with publishing at least six centuries ago.

In the much smaller world of that day the great and mighty were often seen in Fleet Street, especially as it was on the way from royal Westminster to the City of London. De Worde's house was particularly well sited for viewing the pageantry, and the ageing printer would have noted ominous signs of the struggle between King and Pope in the ceremonies he saw in his last days. In 1509 a radiant young Henry VIII with his new queen, Catherine, had passed in procession down Fleet Street. Nearly twenty years later two cardinals, drenched with rain, went together down the same street to Bridewell palace. They were Cardinals Campeggio and Wolsey who were to meet with the King to discuss whether he was legally married to Catherine. And in 1533, another of Henry's queens, Anne Boleyn, traversed the same path on her way to her coronation in splendid procession. Oddly enough a number of abbots rode with her; they were not yet under royal ban. The procession stopped outside de Worde's house and gathered round the conduit, which was specially decorated for the occasion.

Extract from inventory of printing house
Common Plea Roll No. 1156 Michaelmas Term, 1st Mary

Chapter Three

Before considering de Worde's type material it might be as well to define the terms which are used. The following descriptions are based on those given in A. F. Johnson's *Type Designs: Their History and Development* (London, 1959). The figures after some types indicate the number of millimetres occupied by twenty lines.

Textura is the upright and angular letter, which was used for liturgical works north of the Alps and which was copied by Gutenberg. This script with its tall letters, black face and short ascenders and descenders enabled the scribe to produce a closely packed page with a large proportion of black and white, which had the appearance of woven texture – hence the name.

One half of Caxton's types were Texturas and from them are descended those of the first generation of English printers, including de Worde. The traditional 'black letter' or 'English' used in this country and shown in type specimens down to the nineteenth century is a small Textura and differs little from de Worde's type. In the Thorowgood General Specimen there appears: 'This Black is very ancient and was the one generally used by Caxton's apprentice and successor Wynkyn de Worde.' That is not to say, of course, that this 'Black' really was an original de Worde type.[2] Reed's

2 This type, English Black No 3, can be traced to the Grover foundry (late seventeenth century) and may well be of sixteenth-century origin. It is now available as 14-point Ancient Black from Stephenson Blake. In the days before the point system this would have been called English English – the old body size and the old name of the type.

Old English Letter Foundries states that de Worde was, in all probability, the first to import French matrices into this country and to produce a letter which henceforth took the name 'English' as being the national character of our early typography.

Rotunda is a rounded letter with full curves, in contrast to the angularity of Textura. The feet of the Textura have in part disappeared. In England, says Johnson, it was always an alien letter. But both de Worde and Pynson had small Rotundas which they used for notes with their usual Texturas.

Roman types are based on the book hand of the Renaissance humanists. Roman is derived from a script, the Carolingian, which was more ancient than any gothic descendant, but it had been revived by the humanists and was translated into type soon after the invention of printing from movable types. The upper case is at least pure roman and the lower case is an immediate descendant. The name probably originated from the fact that the first roman used in France, that of the Sorbonne Press of 1470, was copied from the fount of Sweynheym and Pannartz used at Rome from 1467.

Wynkyn de Worde's roman letter of 1523 closely resembled contemporary French romans. His first use of the roman letter was in Whittinton's *Syntax* in 1520.

There are two divisions of roman – the formal and the bastard, otherwise italic. Italic is a cursive letter and was so called by its original designers – 'corsiva' or 'cancellaresca', and is still called 'cursiv' by the Germans. The earliest italics were based on the writing hand of the Papal Chancery. They were not originally designed to be a companion letter to roman, but by the close of the sixteenth century there were already indications of this current practice.

Wynkyn de Worde was the first to use italic in England in Wakefield's *Oratio de Laudibus Trium Linguarum* in 1528. It was also the first book printed in England in which Hebrew and Arabic characters appear. These were cut in wood. The author complained that he was compelled to omit a third part because the printer had no Hebrew types. The first appearance of Greek characters in an English printed book is in de Worde's edition of

Whittinton's *De Concinitate Grammatices*, 1517, which were also cut in wood.

Books from Westminster

While at Westminster de Worde contented himself mainly with Caxton's types, although he introduced some of his own. The Caxton 99mm used in *Charles the Great*, 1485, de Worde modified and used in *The Life of St Catherine*. The Caxton 114mm he used in a new edition of *The Golden Legend*. Although this book is dated 20th May 1493 (well after Caxton's death) it contains Caxton's name. De Worde printed it from an earlier edition, merely altering the date, or perhaps he meant the words 'By me William Caxton' to refer to the translation rather than the printing. More likely, however, bearing in mind later printing errors of de Worde's, it was simply a mistake. In *Directorium Sacerdotum* (1495) he used Caxton's 135mm.

In his first two years as a master printer at Westminster de Worde printed five books – *The Book of Courtesy*, the *Treatise of Love*, *The Chastising of God's Children*, *The Life of St Catherine*, and a third edition of *The Golden Legend*.

The Chastising of God's Children is interesting typographically as being the first book printed at Westminster with a title-page. Title-pages were an early development in book printing. The earliest seem to be the work of Fust and Schoeffer in Mainz in 1463 and the earliest in England the work of William de Machlinia about 1490 in *A passing gode lityll boke necessarye & behovefull agenst the Pestilence*. William Caxton had seen no reason to break with manuscript practice and the nature of his publications had to be gathered from the opening words on the second leaf. Caxton may have seen Machlinia's innovation but did not introduce it himself. McKerrow in his *Introduction to Bibliography* writes: 'In the hands of Wynkyn de Worde, however, the title page rapidly developed into a conspicuous feature of the book, and though one or two of his earlier contemporaries never used it, we

¶ The prouffytable boke for manes soule/And right comfor=
table to the body/and specyally in aduersitte gtrybulacyon/Whiche
boke is called The Chastysing of goddes Chyldren

An early form of title page, printed by de Worde, *c.* 1492

find that by the beginning of the sixteenth century some sort of title page is always present.'

At the end of 1493 de Worde's first type (95mm) made its appearance in an edition of John Mirk's *Liber Festivalis* (an oft-printed work from Caxton onwards). It was a clean, easy to read black letter, with very few joined letters. With it went a set of small Lombardic capitals. De Worde used this type often up to 1500, but it lasted only a short time after that date and does not seem to have been used after 1502.

Up to this time de Worde had not put his name to any book, though most of them contain his first device, a copy on a small scale of Caxton's.

In 1494 came a change. He printed two important books, the *Scala Perfectionis* of Walter Hylton, a Carthusian monk, and a reprint of the *Speculum Vitae Christi*. The *Scala Perfectionis* is the first book to which de Worde put his name. It was written and printed for Margaret Beaufort, the mother of the King (Henry VII). This information is given in a poem at the end of the book.

The *Speculum* is interesting because Caxton's small type (81mm) is found in it, the only time it was used in a book, although it had been used for printing indulgences. Caxton used it for an indulgence granted by Innocent VIII; de Worde used it for the same indulgence re-granted by Alexander VI.

Three editions of the *Horae ad usum Sarum*, two in quarto and one in octavo, are ascribed in 1494. Those in quarto contain Caxton borders and woodcuts.

In 1495 there appeared the *Vitas Patrum*, with many badly designed illustrations. It was printed in de Worde's own 95mm type. Then came *Introductorium linguae latinae* and a series of small tracts, including one giving information to pilgrims visiting the Holy Land.

preste singe of requiez as
be didz to fore e so he did
as ofte as he myght

¶Also we fynde that fi
scheris sette her nettes in
þe rueste to fisshe e they to
ke vp a grete pese of Ise
e that hit was the coldis
ste yse that euer they feld
e hit wolde not melte for
the sonne Than brought
they þ yse to the bishop
for he had a grete bren=
nyngz hete in his fete and
hit was the coldiste that
euer he felte Than spake
there a voyce to him out
of the yse y am a soule þ
suffre my penaunce here in
this yse for y haue no fre
des that wolle do masses
for me y shall be delyue=
red of my penaunce and
thow shalt be hole of thy
sikenes e he seyde he wol
de wolde singe for him
e bad telle him his name
e euer while he was atte
masse he leyde the yse vn
der his fete and euer as he
seyde masse the yse malte
awey e so in a while the
yse was molton e the son

le oute of purgatory and
the bishopp was hole of
his sikenesse ¶Thanne the
soule apperid him with
moche ioye e seyde with
thy masses singyng y am
holpyn oute of peyne in
to euer lastyngz blysse. e
he tolde the bishopp that
he shulde dye sone aftyr
e to come to euer lasting
ioye with outyn ende to
the whiche god bryngz
vs all to Amen

De festo sancti martini.

Gode frendis so
che a day ye shall
haue seynte mar=
tens day whann marten
was but iij. yere of age he
cutt his mantell in to pe=
ces as he wer amonge o
thir knyghtis e was not
yit cristoned e gafe hal
fe his mantell to a pore
man for god dis sake that
askid almes than the ny
ghte aftyr god had the
same clothe e seyd to his
angell. Marten that is
not cristoned hathe clo
thid me in this clothe e

E iij

De Worde's first type, used in John Mirk's *Liber Festivalis* 1493

Paper-making mentioned

1495 is the year usually given to the edition of the English translation of the *De proprietatibus rerum*, mentioned earlier.

As well as the reference to Caxton's stay in Cologne, the verse epilogue makes the first known mention of paper-making in England. After remembering Caxton the verse continues:

And Iohn Tate the yonger Ioye mote he broke
Whiche late hathe in Englond doo make this paper thynne
That now in our englyssh this boke is printed Inne

The mark in this paper is an eight-pointed star. Similar paper was used in de Worde's second edition of *The Golden Legend*, dated 8th January, 1498.

John Tate, a Mercer, was the son of John Tate, who was Mayor in 1473. The younger Tate died in 1507 and his will contains several references to his paper mill which was in Hertford. The mill is known to have been at work in 1498 when it was visited by Henry VII.

In 1496 de Worde also produced a reprint of the well-known *Book of St Albans*, a treatise on hunting, hawking and heraldry, with the addition in this issue of a chapter on fishing with an angle, said to be the earliest printed treatise on the art.

It was printed in a foreign type (103mm), a broad square letter, obtained from van Os, a printer of Gouda, who parted with it about 1490, when he removed to Copenhagen. It does not seem to have been used again in England. Writers have puzzled as to why de Worde did not use this type again. There may be a number of reasons of which one was that it was not suitable for English books (Plomer), and naturally there may have been books set in it which have simply not come down to us.

Three fine folios appeared in 1498 – the *Morte d'arthur*, another edition of *The Golden Legend* and the *Canterbury Tales*. The *Morte d'arthur* was a reprint of a Caxton, but with illustrations added. They were very badly

Prohemium Bartholomei
de proprietatibus rerum.

Eternall lawde to god grettest of myghe
He hertely peue of euery creature
Whyche of his goodnesse sendyth grace
To sondry folke as blessyd auenture clyghe
Whoos spyryte of counsell comfortyth full sure
All suche as luste to seke for sapience
And makyth them wyse by grete Intelligence

As thus where men full naturally desyre
Of sondry thynges & meruels for to knowe
Of erthe of ayre of water and of fire
Of erbe & tree whiche groweth bothe hyghe & lowe
And other thynges as nature hath them sowe
Of thyse the knowlege comyth by goddis grace
And of all thynge that realon maye them brace

Whan J beholde the thynges naturall
Gadryd by grace sent from the holy ghost
Breiffely compyled in bokes specyall
As Bartholomewe sheweth & eke declaryth most
Than J reioyce remembrynge euery coste
How some countree hath grete comodite
Some rote some frute some stoon of hyghe degre

Praysed be god whyche hath so well enduyd
The auctor wyth grace de proprietatibus
To se so many naturall thynges renewyd
Whiche in his boke he hath compyled thus
Where thrugh bylredynge we maye comfort vs
And wyth conceytes dyuers fede our mynde
As bokes emprynttd she wyth ryght as we fynde

By Wynken de Worde whyche thrugh his dyligena
Emprentyd hath at prayer and desyre
Of Roger Thorney mercer and from thens
This mocion sprange to sette the hertes on fyre
Of suche a loue to rede in euery shyre
Dyuers maters in vodoynge ydylnesse

First part of the Prohemium at the end of *De proprietatibus
rerum*

produced, leading us to think that there could not have been many skilled woodcutters in England at this time.

The colophon of *The Golden Legend* has a line missing, and yet it was reprinted in exactly the same way in later editions issued by de Worde and Julian Notary.

The colophon also shows that de Worde, for some reason, calculated the year as we would do, and not with the early practice of beginning the year on 25th March.

In 1499 de Worde brought out an edition of *Mandeville's Travels*, the first with illustrations. Now he seems to have got busier, confirming the idea that the lawsuit had held him up, and probably also stimulating the idea of a move to Fleet Street. While the dated books known to us never rise above four in the earlier years, in 1499 there are ten. De Worde reprinted a Caxton book, *the Horse, the Shepe, and the Ghoos* which had a leaf missing, leaving the leaf out and making nonsense of all that followed. This seems to confirm how rushed he was becoming. In April 1499 he first used his two Rotunda types (93mm and 53mm) in Ioannes *de Garlandia Equiuoca*. The 93mm is frequently found in the sixteenth century de Worde books and the 53mm is usually used for marginal notes.

There is no doubt that de Worde understood the popular market. He seldom printed a book without illustrations, even if sometimes they were badly done.

To brighten up a book he would use the same woodcut more than once. He did this in John Lydgate's *The assemble of the goddes* (1498) using at both beginning and end a woodcut showing most ungodlike figures seated round a table. It was a woodcut from Caxton's second edition of Chaucer's *Canterbury Tales*, and is an appropriate illustration for that book – the various characters are recognisable. But any illustration was better than none for de Worde – and anyway who is to say what the ancient gods looked like? In *A right profytable tretyse compendiously drawn out of many and dyvers wrytungs of holy men* by Thomas Betson (1500) (a kind of early religious digest) he used a famous block of the Crucifixion at both beginning and end. This is the book with the injunction to the reader to 'lerne to kepe your bokes clene'. Unfortunately the exhortation loses some of its effect by the fact that the 'n' in 'clene' is printed upside down.

At the time of his move to Fleet Street he seems to have got rid of a considerable portion of his stock, for many of the cuts belonging to Caxton or de Worde are found afterwards in books printed by Julian Notary. The number of known titles printed by de Worde at Westminster is estimated at 110.

Publications after 1500

After 1500 de Worde used only two of his fifteenth-century types. In the sixteenth century he had eight Texturas (blacks), one Rotunda or round text, two romans and two italics, and except for two Texturas, including the earlier of the two fifteenth-century types, all can be traced to a French or Low Countries source. He made some alterations in one of his Textura types, using three different s's and three w's in the course of time. These alterations may have been made in his own foundry, as English printers would find no w in a French fount and were forced to cut their own.

Any conclusions about the operations of early printers as typefounders are conjectural, but it is probable that Caxton possessed very rough materials for casting type. De Worde made frequent use of Caxton's No 3 type (135mm) and this seems to point to the existence of the matrices as well as the types in this country. Textura 95mm is the most frequently found of all de Worde's types in the sixteenth century. From time to time some of the letters were re-cut and the small differences form an approximate guide for the dating of undated books. His Rotunda was the only one of its kind used by de Worde.

The year 1501 was mostly taken up with settling into his new premises. His output was small, and only one book is known to have been issued that year – *Mons Perfectionis*.

Wynkyn de Worde's output during the following years was moulded by popular taste and by foreign competition. He produced ballads, jest books, romances and chap books, often only known from fragments, which have survived in old bindings. We cannot estimate the number which have perished.

This is a problem which always faces bibliographers. Popular printed material is obviously more prone to destruction than that which is printed for special occasions or for a limited class of people. For example, de Worde would have known that the *Book of St Albans* appealed specially to the richer classes and struck off copies on vellum. Some of these have come down to us today.

The public, and hence de Worde, was very fond of almanacks and prognostications, which purported to tell the future. *Old Moore's Almanack* is still popular today. The earliest English prognostication of which there is any mention was one by Jasper Laet of Antwerp, 'printed by Caxton in 1493'. If the date is correct it must, of course, have been printed by de Worde. Only three prognostications are understood to remain from the fifteenth century, and then in fragments. One is a de Worde fragment consisting of two leaves of a translation of one of William Parron's prognostications for 1498. The year was not a good one for kings to make journeys, apparently.

There is also a fragment of a de Worde prognostication for 1523. In 1508 he issued an Almanack for twelve years, a 32mo, and the smallest book he printed. It was issued for popular use, perhaps by travellers or mariners. Another in 1522 was for fifteen years.

The year 1509 was an important one for de Worde. The death of Henry VII was soon followed by that of his patroness, the Countess of Richmond. However, the output of books was the largest in any year of his life. The royal funerals and the following coronation would no doubt have attracted crowds to London and increased business. In the year de Worde produced a very large number of popular poems and stories, among them such books as *Rychard Cuer de Lion*, *The Conversion of Swerers*, *The Fifteen Joys of Marriage*, *The Parliament of Devils*, and Hawe's *Pastime of Pleasure*.

libri ca. vj. vel ﬨ﬩﬷ marcheſhuan october ﬥﬖ﬷
kiſleſ nouēber, zachariȩ ca. vij. & Machabeoꝝ
primo. ﬨ﬜ﬨ Teueth december. Eſter. ca. ij. Hie
ronymus in cōmētarijs ſup. xxix. Eʒechielis
caput, iſm interpretaꝛ Ianuari⁹, ﬦﬗﬖ ſheuat
Ianuarius zachariȩ ca. j. ﬥﬖﬧﬧﬨﬖ Adar riſhon
februari⁹, Eſter. ca. ix. ﬨﬖﬧ﬷ ueadar vꝉꞌﬥﬖ ﬨﬖ
Adar ſheni. Pirchon i radice Bul hȩc mēſiū noia aſſe
rēs eē Perſica ſic ſubiūgit. Sed ligua ſācta di,
cit, mēſis primus, ad menſē ſecūdum, in mēſe
tertio Vencemar tſum harcuij ſhehu tammuz uetſum bachamio
ſhi Aſ uetſum hahaſiri ſhehu Teueth aual korin lahē kemo ſhek,
korin lahen hem haggoijm ſhennithhaěuu bahen kamchi itē
hȩc mēſiū noia negat hebraica eſſe, in cōmēta
arijs ſup. xxiiij. Eʒechie. ca. Vbi hȩc hʒ verba
en ſhemoth leiamim bilſhon hakkodeſh ella leniiſpar ieme haſh,
ſhabbath kemo beachadh heſhabbath biſhni beſhabbath uechule
uelo lachodaſhim ella riſhon ſheni ſheliſhi, hoc eſt, non ſūt
nomina ſeptem diebus hebdomadæ propria,
in lingua ſancta ſicut apud gentes ſed a nu=
mero dierū ſabbati denoiationem accipiunt
ſic, prima ſabbati, ſecunda ſabbati, tertia ſab=
bati. &c. Neꝗ mēſibus, niſi primus, ſecūdus,
tertius. &c. At iam iuxta pollicitationē ab ini=
tio de Arabica aliquid dicem⁹. ⸿ Phœnices
(de quibus Lucanus, primi fame ſi crediꝛ auſi,
māſurā rudibus vocem ſignare figuris) pœ=
ni vel poti⁹ phœni, Aphri (qui phœnicū liguā
nōnulla ex parte corruperūt) Mauri, harabes
(apud quos πο⸒μϖⲓ⸒ pingueſcūt muſica magis q̄

Res mirifica.

First use of italic type in England by de Worde in *Oratio de Laudibus
Trium Linguarum*, 1528. It was also the first book in which Hebrew and
Arabic characters appear, cut in wood

The côuercyon of Swerers.

Title page, *Conversion of Swerers*, 1509

Perhaps the most interesting was the edition of Henry Watson's version of *The Ship of Fools*.

In the few books printed between the death of Henry VII and the Countess of Richmond de Worde calls himself printer to the King's grandmother.

Grammatical works

De Worde continued to print popular works, including books of riddles and romantic histories, but in 1512 began the first of the grammatical works of Whittinton, whose various works became so popular that de Worde sometimes issued as many as four editions of one work a year. Robert Whittinton was a schoolmaster and the printing of his grammars occupied de Worde for more than twenty years and few other printers ventured to disturb his virtual monopoly. De Worde also printed books for other grammarians. The illustrations for his edition of Holt's *Lac Puerorum* are an early example of visual aids to the learning of Latin.

So busy was de Worde in his lifetime as printer-publisher that other printers worked for him. Julian Notary and his partners printed as early as 1497 an edition of the *Horae ad usum Sarum* for de Worde. The next year they printed a Sarum Missal at his command and expense. Notary had started up in London, had moved to Westminster in 1498, and back to London almost immediately after de Worde. He worked near Temple Bar so was almost certainly in close touch with his fellow master printer.

In 1522 an edition of the *Mirror of Gold for the sinful soul* appeared with de Worde's name in the colophon but Duff thinks that it was printed for him by John Skot . . . 'an examination of several of de Worde's books about this time shows that they were also produced by Skot'.

The first genuine music book printed by de Worde was the *Book of Songs* in 1530. In *The Earliest English Music Printing* (London, 1903) Robert Steele writes: 'The two-print music of Wynkyn de Worde in 1530 has staves which have every appearance of being printed from metal blocks.

The notes were printed at the same time as the text, and are in excellent register. They are well designed, but do not seem to have been used again. By a fortunate accident, one large capital has been printed over the lines, but apart from this the different tones of the inks show sufficiently that they were separately printed. It is curious, considering how bad a printer Wynkyn de Worde was, that this book is the best piece of music printing of the century. The type is evidently modelled on the Augsburg type of Oeglin (1507).'

This writer repeats the charge that de Worde was a bad printer, again forgetting to take circumstances into account. Possibly de Worde was able to spend more time than usual over the *Book of Songs*. We must remember also that by this date he was an old and prosperous citizen who had no need to do rushed work. In fact, from this time on much of his work was confined to re-printing earlier editions and only about one in twenty were new books. A good deal of his work was done by other printers and in his last few years he began printing work for other people. In other words, in his old age he probably lacked the urge to forage for new and exciting manuscripts to print.

For his old apprentice, John Bydell, he printed four or five books in 1533 and 1534. De Worde's last book was a little poem *The Complaint of those too soon maryed*. He had himself been married more than fifty-five years before, but his wife had long been dead.

Chapter Four

De Worde lived in an era when the structure of society was being trans-formed, but he missed seeing a great change come over Fleet Street and over the conduct of religious services in his church. He died in 1535 just before the dissolution of the religious houses by Henry VIII. This brought about the end of the great establishment of the Dominicans at Blackfriars and the smaller house of the Carmelites at Whitefriars. The bishops' establishments were broken up and the whole character of the street altered.

De Worde is presumed to have been quite old when he died (old, that is, for a man in the sixteenth century – in his late seventies), and the changes which were taking place, not only in religion, but in the status of the foreign printer in England may have caused him concern.

The foreign printer was a necessity to England when the trade was introduced. In the year 1484 important acts were passed relating to foreign traders, but special exemption was made for those connected with the book trade.

This exemption, which was not repealed until 1534, gave absolute liberty to foreign printers and stationers to trade and reside in England. De Worde was probably an honoured man in his youth as he could exercise the 'crafte of pryntynge', and the exemption may explain why he did not take out letters of denization until 1496, when he had presumably been in England for twenty years. A denizen was a foreigner admitted to residence

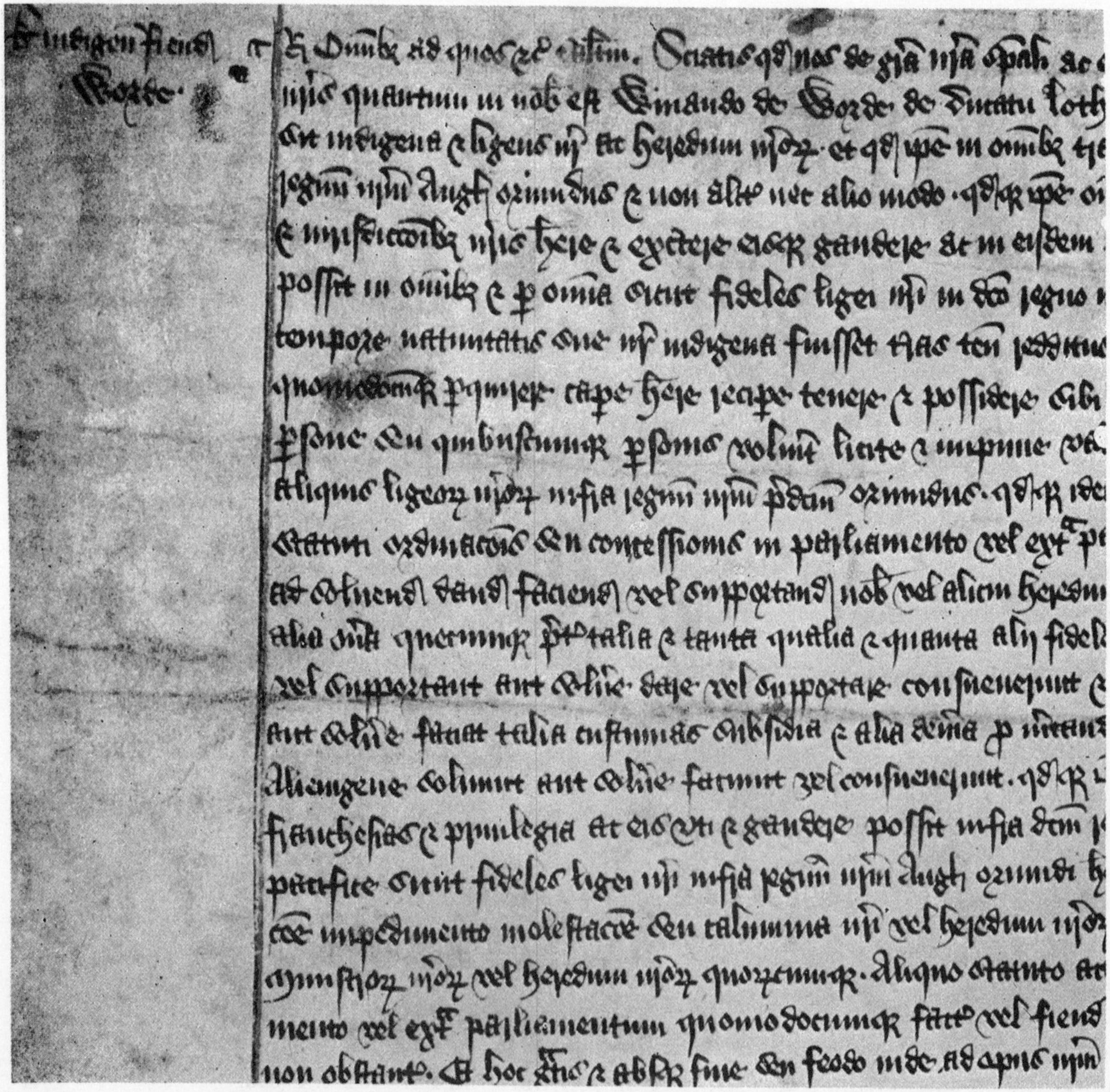

Wynkyn de Worde's letters of denization

and certain rights. Though the immigration of foreigners had been encouraged by the Government it evoked hostility from native craftsmen and was the frequent cause of fights and squabbles. For example, Richard Pynson, a Norman, de Worde's friendly rival, made 'lamentable compleynt' to Cardinal Morton, in the Star Chamber, of riotous assembly and assault committed upon him and his servants on the 21st April 1500. This may have been the reason for his removal from St Clement Danes into Fleet Street and the comparatively greater security of the Mayor's jurisdiction.

Perhaps de Worde had seen the way the wind was blowing in 1496, for a series of restrictive regulations on foreign printers began in 1523, whereby all aliens were prohibited from having any but English apprentices and were also forbidden to employ more than two foreign journeymen. In 1529 another Act prohibited the setting up of a press by any alien, and, finally, in 1534 (the year before de Worde's death) the exemption was lifted completely, it being pointed out there were few books and few printers in the realm when it was given in the first year of Richard III, but now many of the King's 'natural subjects' had diligently learned to exercise the craft and had to be protected.

Relations with other printers

Towards the end of 1508 when Pynson was appointed printer to the King, de Worde appears to have received some sort of official appointment as printer to the Countess of Richmond, the King's mother. He had printed several books before this time at her request but he had not called himself her printer. Perhaps Pynson's new appointment prompted de Worde to ask for the new title.

It is interesting to consider the relations between de Worde and Pynson. Mr Bennett says that the history of printing during the first three decades of the sixteenth century is largely the history of these two men, for they outdistanced all rivals who from time to time appeared. In the first decade they were responsible for 70 per cent of the entire output of books in

English; in the next decade 73 per cent, and in the third decade 55 per cent.

While both printed books of every kind, particularly religious works, each of them specialised to some extent. De Worde paid attention to books required for the grammar schools while Pynson tried to meet the needs of lawyers.

Literary piracy was frequently practised in that age but in 1507 de Worde and Pynson tried co-operation instead of competition and shared an edition of *The Boke Royal* which de Worde printed. This is the first example in England of the combination of firms in the book trade. Despite their rivalry de Worde and Pynson did frequent business together. De Worde had a far larger stock of woodcuts than Pynson and Pynson is often found borrowing cuts from him.

The printers of the day, small in number, must have known each other well and worked together. It is also obvious that since there were very few shops in which to learn the trade the apprentices who eventually became masters nearly all knew each other in youth.

De Worde seems to have been intimately connected with York printers. A Dutchman, Gerard Freez, or Vries, a York stationer, who changed his name to Wandsforth, died in 1510 and in his will left de Worde forty shillings in payment of a debt. In 1509 de Worde asserts in a colophon that he printed an edition of the York manual for two stationers John Gachet and James Ferrebouc, but the book looks as if it were printed in Paris for de Worde.

Hugo Goes, York's first known printer, printed in 1509 a *Directorium* of York in an early discarded type of Wynkyn de Worde's. De Worde seems to have done business with Goes, and Duff thinks that Henry Watson, who was associated with Goes, was de Worde's assistant of that name.

De Worde also knew York's second printer, Ursyn Mylner. In 1516 Mylner issued a Whittinton grammar. His device consisted of a shield hanging from a tree supported by a bear, an allusion to the name Ursyn, and an ass. The shield is divided per pale and bears in one half a windmill and in the other a sun. The mill is obviously for Mylner and the sun may refer to a business partnership with de Worde, the main printer of Whittinton's works. In any case, the book contains a woodcut used by de Worde in grammar books.

De Worde also had connections with Oxford. He printed the *Formalitates* of Antonius Sirectus for Henry Jacobi, a London stationer who had migrated to Oxford. When John Scolar started up Oxford's second press in 1517 de Worde supplied some of the type and woodcuts for his first books, the type being that used for Jacobi's book by Sirectus.

Warning against heresy

De Worde did not escape his share of the political and religious problems of the period. In 1524 he was one of those warned by Bishop Tunstall against importing Lutheran books into England. Any new books received by him from abroad were to be submitted for approval either to the Lord Cardinal, the Archbishop of Canterbury, the Bishop of London, or the Bishop of Rochester.

A year later he was again summoned before the bishop with John Gough to answer a charge of having published a work called *The Image of Love*. De Worde confessed that he was one of those present in the previous year and that since that date he had printed *The Image of Love*, which was alleged to contain heresy, and had sent sixty copies to the nuns of Syon and had sold as many more. The two men were warned not to sell any more and to get back those they had already sold.

Chapter Five

After a long and busy life Wynkyn de Worde died in the early days of 1535 and, like his master Caxton, left no heir. His will is dated 5th June 1534. In it he is described as citizen and stationer. The Stationers Company have no record going back to that period and was not incorporated until 1557 (Philip and Mary). But he may well have been a member of the company, and there is some evidence that he may have been of the Leathersellers Company also. To the Fraternity of Our Blessed Lady of St Bride's Church, of which he was a brother, he left ten shillings to pray for his soul.

He asked that his body be buried before the high altar of St Katherine in the Church of St Bride. During the excavations at St Bride's Church, following its partial destruction in the second world war, and before its re-building, some remains were found which may well be those of Wynkyn de Worde. Consisting of a part of a skull, some bones and lead from a coffin, they were found where it is known the altar of St Katherine stood. But they may equally be those of James Gaver, one of de Worde's servants, who continued to live with another of de Worde's servants, Bydell, at the sign of the Sun after de Worde's death. Gaver died in 1545 and in his will he requested that he might be buried in St Bride's Church before the altar of St Katherine 'neare unto Wynkyn de Worde sometyme my master'.

De Worde made bequests to various of his servants, mostly in printed books, to Nowell, the bookbinder in Shoe Lane (whom Mr Duff has identi-fied as Noel Havy, a Frenchman), to each of his apprentices, and forgave

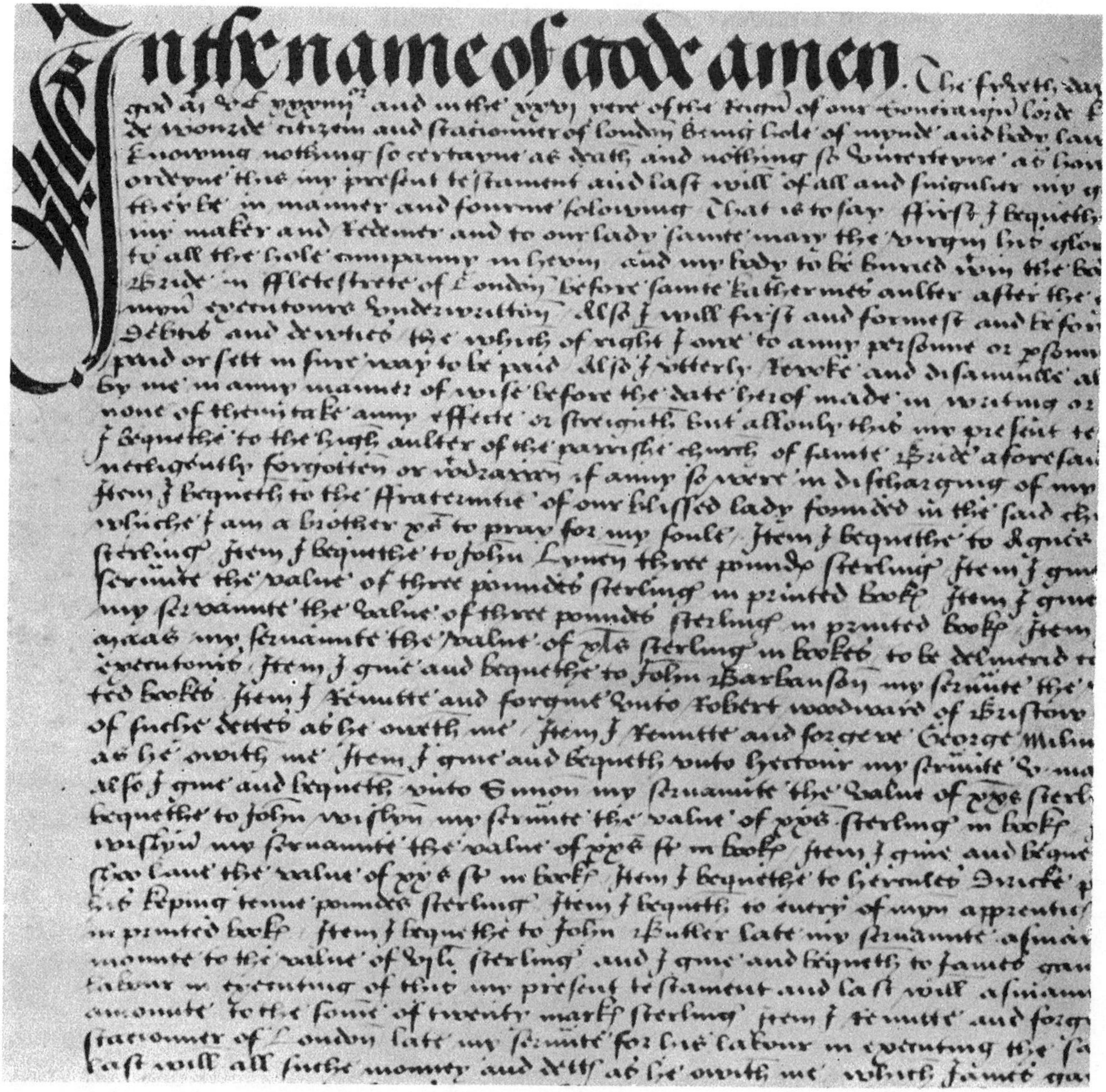

In the name of god amen

An extract from de Worde's will

debts of a number of persons. John 'Bedill' and James Gaver were the executors and as overseers he named Henry Pepwell, John Gough and Robert Copland, to whom he also made bequests. The witnesses were Humphry Town 'curat', John Studd, Thomas Cooke and John Tourner.

He instructed his executors to purchase land near London, the income from which was to be spent in an obit for his soul and in a yearly gift of twenty shillings to the poor of the parish of St Bride's.

The nature of de Worde's business

That de Worde was a bookseller as well as a printer is apparent. Like other early printers he made his own ink and probably cast his own types (although this does not necessarily mean that he cut punches). Of his work as a bookbinder we know little.

Some indication of de Worde's activities can be gauged from an inventory attached to the details of a legal action taken in 1553 against the printers William and Humphrey Powell by William Towley. Plomer has identified the inventory as being that of de Worde's house at the sign of the Sun. Towley, he thinks, was acting as the agent for Edward Whitchurch, the Protestant printer, who occupied the house after John Bydell and James Gaver. Anticipating trouble in the new reign of the Catholic Queen Mary he disposed of the printing house to William and Humphrey Powell. Apparently they failed to carry out their contract, and Whitchurch brought an action to recover the chattels. The details are in the Common Plea Roll 1156, Michaelmas Term, 1st Mary. Plomer identifies the house from the fact that the plaintiffs recovered against the Powells and the business passed into the hands of John Wayland who used a Whitchurch device in 1554; and also from the fact that the bulk of the books in the inventory were printed by Wynkyn de Worde 'and where should these be found, but on the premises he once occupied?' He says that when John Bydell, one of de Worde's executors, moved into the house he quite conceivably took over the premises as it stood. The same thing may have happened when Whitchurch succeeded Bydell, though no doubt each of them added something of his own.

This is plausible, and whether or not the inventory, which is definite enough, was actually that of 'the Sun' it does show what a printer had as equipment less than twenty years after de Worde's death, and might reasonably be the type of equipment possessed by de Worde.

The inventory was written partly in Latin, partly in French and partly in English. This was not the work of a clerk, says Plomer, but possibly of foreign workmen working at the house at the time. After the stock of books there follows: 'vnū le sowyng presse 13 les bordes voc. shelfes quatuor les pryntyng presses duo par de cases wythe letters to prynte cu pyctures & historiis quatuordecem par del wood (   ) decem les bordes to lay-vppon paper duo lez deles formes one longe & nother shorte tres lez pottes for pryntynge Ink duo Ink blak boxes wythe a redde boxe duos boxes of canon of grete Roman duo le Forme of Inglysshe letter sett in a chase one forme of the grete primer letter sett in a chase one forme of pica bownde vp in pagies duo forme of the longe primer letter in pages vnū le shelffe vnū le baskett vnū le baskett vnū le boxe full of stykes for the presses cum diversis aliis rebus circa le pryntynge howse vnū parr del empty cases vnū lapidem cu vno lemuller to grynde colours wytheall vnū le box cum grete woodden letters duo parr of cases wythe letters, septem basketts with letters vnū le forme and di of a new pye letter duo les shelfes cum picturis, quatuor par del Iren chases vnū le baskett full of old letters cum diversis aliis rebuz circa landem domum, vnū librum voca Grayle in pchement vnū le stole cu divers chaseis del woodd cum par del trestles dicers Instrument cum Tolis to bynde wythe duos les olde Tubbes vnū le ladell et certum parvum metallum, vnū le playnge presse cum diversis les bordes vnū vetus ciphum, vnū le trowghe plumbeis duo les barrells cu atramento in eis, tres lez virkyns cum sale in eis, quadraginta & sex bounde bookes wyth dyvers sortes of olde bookes in quayers librum de intro-duccione ad sapienciam 50 libros of the preparacyon of the dethe of Erasmus.'

The inventory points clearly to a bindery, and the 'Grayle in parchment' might be a manuscript awaiting printing. The 'pictures and historiis' might refer to wood blocks.

What is most interesting is the reference to four printing presses, which might be a further pointer to the fact that they were de Worde's. It was a large number for a printer of those days to have, but de Worde's output would justify it. Moreover the reference to 'le ladell et certum parvum metallum' and 'le trowghe plumbeis' point to a foundry.

De Worde inherited Caxton's binding stamps with the rest of his printing material. Duff says he found in a college library in Oxford a book with these stamps, evidently bound by de Worde and the boards were lined with waste leaves of three books printed by him, one being unknown and one by Caxton. De Worde's bindings are the least easily identified of any of the fifteenth century, for beyond these few dies of Caxton's there are none that can definitely be ascribed to him, and even the various bindings that might be ascribed to him from the fragments found in them, vary so much in style and decoration that it seems impossible that they could have all come from one shop.

We know from de Worde's will that he employed several binders. He left bequests to Alard, bookbinder, his servant, to Nowel, the bookbinder in Shoe Lane, where bookbinders abounded, and James Gaver, who was one of his executors, was one of the large family of Gavere, binders in the Low Countries.

An additional reason for de Worde's move to Fleet Street and particularly the vicinity of Shoe Lane may have been the desire to be near a centre of bookbinding, a necessity if he were to launch out on a big scale as a publisher. It looks as if he had a small bindery of his own but also put work out.

De Worde used no less than fourteen different devices, as recorded by McKerrow in his book *Printers' and Publishers' Devices in England and Scotland, 1485–1640*. At first he used versions of Caxton's mark, and continued to incorporate Caxton's initials in his own. From the state of his devices it is possible to approximately date his undated books.

Chapter Six

What was de Worde's influence on the popular press? He arrived at a time when there had been a rapid growth of vernacular manuscripts to meet a great variety of needs. From Caxton onwards printers were aware of the desire for books and texts on all kinds of practical matters as well as upon religion, legal and scientific topics.

In addition to lacking Caxton's scholarly outlook de Worde also had not the contacts with the aristocracy which had been so important an influence on Caxton's output. The move to Fleet Street indicates that de Worde probably sensed that his future lay among the smaller people than with the upper classes.

H. S. Bennett gives us an excellent estimate of de Worde's position.

The following passage from his book is particularly worth quoting: 'For forty years then from the death of Caxton until about 1532 de Worde and Pynson were the overwhelmingly important figures in the printing industry. How had they exercised their power? We have seen how each of them specialised to some extent, and Pynson's appointment as the King's Printer about 1508–9 meant that he had to use his resources when so commanded to print proclamations, books of statutes, etc. Nevertheless, each of them can look back on a body of publications touching very many interests and offering something for every literary appetite. Here we part company to some extent, with the bibliographers and students of typography who have allowed their admiration of Pynson's superior press work to mask the debt we owe to de Worde for the mass and variety of his output. Gordon Duff says that de Worde was "not skilful as a printer", while H. R. Plomer accuses him of a lack of artistic feeling in his choice and arrangement of woodcuts, of stupid mistakes and carelessness in composition and press work and being a man of no literary taste. We must readily admit all of this, although Plomer's last phrase is a little hard, and at the same time assert that de Worde's services to literature, to religion and to the popularisation of the printed word were very considerable.'

Magnitude of output

Mr Bennett points out the magnitude of de Worde's output between 1492 and 1532 – his imprint appearing on more than 700 works. He says we may estimate de Worde's achievement in another way when we recall that the total number of works recorded in the *Short Title Catalogue* before 1557 is about 5,000, so that de Worde contributed some 15 per cent of this total. He also points out that if it were not for de Worde, far fewer works would have survived. As far as he can judge, by an examination of a sample of de Worde's output at various times, 70 per cent of the books printed by him were printed for the first time. Their names recall a number of items famous in literary history while many have survived only in de Worde's edition. More than 200 works printed by de Worde were never reprinted before 1640 and most of them have never been reprinted at all. While many of the works are of small value as masterpieces they are important items of evidence in the history of taste and in the investigation of the growth and appetite of the early reading public. But not all of de Worde's pioneer editions can be written off as of comparatively little value. In the field of romance literature we find that de Worde had a real understanding of what was required. He printed fifteen romances in all and of these twelve appear for the first time under his imprint and three of these – *Apollonius of Tyre* (1510), *Melusine* (1510?), and *Olyuer of Castylle* (1518) – are unique. He had little literary judgment of his own and relied on his friends and helpers such as Robert Copland and Henry Watson for advice, but whatever his methods, his solid contribution to our literature cannot be gainsaid.

De Worde as a printer

What is there to say about the suggestion that de Worde was a bad printer? Firstly, it is not entirely true. He often printed well in good black letter, tightly composed, and he could print large books. He printed the then best available general history of the world, Higden's *Polychronicon*, running to 900 folio pages, in 1495. Even Duff comments favourably on the small neat black letter of his *Manipulus Curatorum* of 1502, and Plomer calls *The Orchard of Syon* (1519) 'a handsome folio'.

Secondly, much of the criticism has been about the woodcuts he used. He has been criticised for letting crude woodcuts through, and for not improving the art of wood cutting. This art was in its early stages in England, and that was hardly de Worde's fault. It was more advanced on the Continent, and when de Worde had the chance of using a well-executed woodcut he did so. He used that of the Crucifixion, which Caxton is thought to have commissioned on the Continent, so much that it wore out. In *The Abbaye of the Holy Ghost* (? 1496) it is a striking piece of work. It was also used in the *Meditation of St Bernard* the same year. The cut began to show signs of wear in 1497, and is an important factor today in determining the date of printing of any undated book in which it is found. The Thomas Betson digest is dated at 1500, not only by the state of the printer's device, but by the cut of the Crucifixion. There is a crack through the rump of a horse and through part of the Cross.

We must appreciate de Worde's quandary. As always, illustrated works were popular. There were few native wood cutters. He therefore used what he could. Sometimes he was lucky. In *A treatyse of Fysshynge wyth an angle*, which was part of the *Book of St Albans* and which appears to have been printed as a separate pamphlet also in 1496, there is a perfectly good woodcut of an angler, even if the perspective of the tub beside him is a little odd. The book is printed in good black ink and there are neat little woodcuts throughout showing tools, rods, lines, hooks and floats.

Thirdly, we must remember that, in the main, de Worde was not printing for posterity. Much of his work was ephemeral, just as is the newspaper and periodical of today.

Finally, we must consider him against the background of early printing. Work took place in cramped, darkened surroundings (there were no Factory Acts). The presses were primitive, the home-made ink was often very thin by modern conceptions. Type had often to be contrived from existing sorts, particularly in England. There was not enough type to print a book all at one time, and work was often done by candlelight. Those who have worked in a small printing shop with limited resources will be more sympathetic towards de Worde than those who do not know what it is to work against time or to pick for sorts of a particular type. When he had the leisure, de Worde could print well, but when he had to get out a pamphlet which was going to sell 'like hot cakes', considerations of fine setting and press work went by the board.

Much of de Worde's life falls into that period of early printing when there was much novelty about the craft and when there was comparative freedom of publication. De Worde's large and varied output owes something to this fact. But after the first quarter of the sixteenth century that freedom began to be menaced not only by acts against foreign printers but strangely enough by the 'New Learning', the teachings of Luther and other reformers. The type of work published by the early printers was superseded by religious and doctrinal quarrelling in print which brought down the heavy hand of authority. The last years of Henry VIII's reign were anxious ones for printers. Nobody could foretell what was safe to print. Books which one year were condemned were later issued with the king's authority. Philip and Mary finally adopted an ingenious method of controlling what was printed by issuing a charter to the Stationers Company forbidding anyone to print who did not belong to it, and, in their turn, they kept a firm grasp on the company. But de Worde had been dead for some twenty years when this happened.

The man himself

What kind of a man was de Worde? What we know of him is mainly from his own works, and there is little outside testimony. But it is clear that his life was one of long and industrious labour, for which he was rewarded in the economic sense. He was obviously a good business man. By paying attention to what the public wanted he avoided the fate of some of the early printers, who produced large quantities of the classics, which sold only in small quantities, and who were thus forced to throw themselves on the mercies of patrons. However, it is not too far fetched to say that he was also a kindly and loyal man.

Unlike other early printers he was a printer by origin. Caxton was a merchant, others were clerics or had been connected with other trades. De Worde almost certainly began his real working life in printing and owed a great deal to Caxton, whom he affectionately remembered throughout the rest of his life. Is it too much to suggest that it was not mere convenience that prompted the continued use of Caxton's initials in his devices but an outward sign of his appreciation of what he owed to England's first printer?

In turn, de Worde was clearly respected by his apprentices, who refer to him in affectionate terms. Perhaps it was a mere pious convention that they did so but it must have been something more than that for James Gaver to ask to be buried near him.

De Worde probably had no strong political or religious views not in accord with authority. As a foreigner this would not have been wise in any case. But all indications are that he kept his nose to the grindstone and did not interest himself in wider issues. If he did print a heretical book he did it innocently for other persons.

Caxton had been a close adherent of the House of York but must have made his peace with Henry VII. De Worde probably knew about the dynastic upheavals of the Wars of the Roses (his own country, Lorraine, had not been free from similar troubles) but he probably preferred the strong government of the Tudor king to any adherence to lost causes.

When Henry VII became king by conquest at Bosworth, in 1485, a new era in English history began. Henry married the heiress of the rival house, Elizabeth of York, and began to repair the ravages of the Wars of the Roses. Most of the great feudal houses had been shattered and Henry made sure that his new middle-class servants had the ascendancy over the old nobles. The feudal age was over. The new king was in favour of commerce. So was de Worde, and during Henry's long reign of twenty-four years he flourished, and laid the foundations of commercial publishing.

Bibliography

T. C. Hansard	*Typographia*. London, 1825. Baldwin, Craddock and Joy.
William Blades	*The Biography and Typography of William Caxton*. London, 1877. Trübner & Co.
Robert Steele	*The Earliest English Music Printing*. London, 1903. Bibliographical Society.
E. Gordon Duff	*The Printers, Stationers and Bookbinders of Westminster and London from 1476 to 1537*. Cambridge, 1906. Cambridge University Press.
R. B. McKerrow	*Printers and Publishers Devices in England and Scotland 1485–1640*. London, 1913. Bibliographical Society.
W. G. Bell	*Fleet Street in Seven Centuries*. London, 1912. Sir Isaac Pitman and Sons Ltd.
Henry R. Plomer	*Wynkyn de Worde and his Contemporaries*. London, 1925. Grafton & Co.
Henry Thomas	*Evidence that the First English Printer learned his craft at Cologne*. London, 1928. Lanston Monotype Corporation.
F. S. Isaac	*English and Scottish Printing Types* 1501–35; 1508–41. The Bibliographical Society. Oxford University Press, 1930.
H. S. Bennett	*English Books and Readers* 1475–1557. Cambridge, 1952. Cambridge University Press.
T. B. Reed	*A History of the Old English Letter Foundries*. London, 1957. Faber and Faber Ltd.
A. F. Johnson	*Type Designs: Their History and Development*. London, 1959. Grafton & Co.

Index